Now you know how your business will work, who will be involved in making it happen, and what relationships you have to develop. Next in 'Launch Your Own Successful Creative Business' you'll find out how to get your message to your customers, and make sure that the finances make business sense.

The main areas you'll cover include:

Marketing Mix
The 7Ps of marketing and how to apply them for your business needs

Marketing Plan
The main elements you need to consider when planning marketing activities

Financial Modelling
Including the vital role of cash flow to ensure your business makes enough money to continue trading in the way you desire.

02

WHAT IS MARKETING?

According to the Chartered Institute of Marketing: **Marketing is the management process responsible for identifying, anticipating and satisfying customer requirements profitably.**

When you're in business, you need to sell your goods or services. And you need someone to buy them. You also have to be seen and heard in a noisy and busy marketplace. It doesn't matter whether you're Bill Gates or a one-man business, the techniques you need to apply to make sure you sell well, profitably and to the right customers are the same.

This section introduces the 7Ps of Marketing. These are also known as the Marketing Mix. It then goes on to describe how to devise a marketing plan.

THE MARKETING MIX

The 7Ps of Marketing

These can help ensure your product or service is in alignment with your company's business and marketing plans. They are:

- 01 **Product**
- 02 **Place**
- 03 **Price**
- 04 **Promotion**
- 05 **People**
- 06 **Process**
- 07 **Physical Environment**

01 Product

Your product or service must appeal to your potential customers, meeting a defined need and, ideally, result in multiple, repeat purchases. You have to ensure there is demand for your product and state what is unique about it.

03

Establishing Demand

However good you think your product is, if no one wants to buy it then no amount of marketing activity will entice them to do so. You may personally love Anchovy and Caper ice cream, but you'd want to test its popularity among potential customers before setting up a business.

Understanding your customers' needs and desires is crucial to the success of your business. Some simple, cost effective market testing will help you identify, at an early stage, if there is a demand by answering a few basic questions:

- Is there a market/desire for your product?
- Is there a satisfactory demand for the product?

You covered much of this in handbook 02, researching your customer.

The USP of a Product

The 'Unique Selling Proposition' of a product or service states clearly the features and benefits that make your product different from your competitors. For example, is it more energy efficient? Made of better quality materials? Does it last longer? Is it more prestigious? Or the only one of its kind on the market?

Your product may share certain features with similar items, for example, all fruit drinks include fruit and are drinkable. The unique benefit of your product may be that it's proven to improve your skin. This would be your USP if it's the only fruit drink on the market that can do this.

The USP can change as the business evolves and different USPs can exist for different types of products and customers.

04

THE MARKETING MIX

02 Place

Place refers to where your product or service is sold to customers. As well as thinking about the location where sales are made, you also have to consider how well your product or service is distributed, which will also have an impact on cost.

If you use intermediaries such as wholesalers, resellers or sales agents, they'll need paying. This is generally included in their mark-up. You will also have to consider how you'll promote the product or service to reach end users.

If the product's large, then you also need to consider storage costs. Your pricing strategy will therefore be affected by:

— Price of production/delivery
— Profit margin
— Storage and stock control

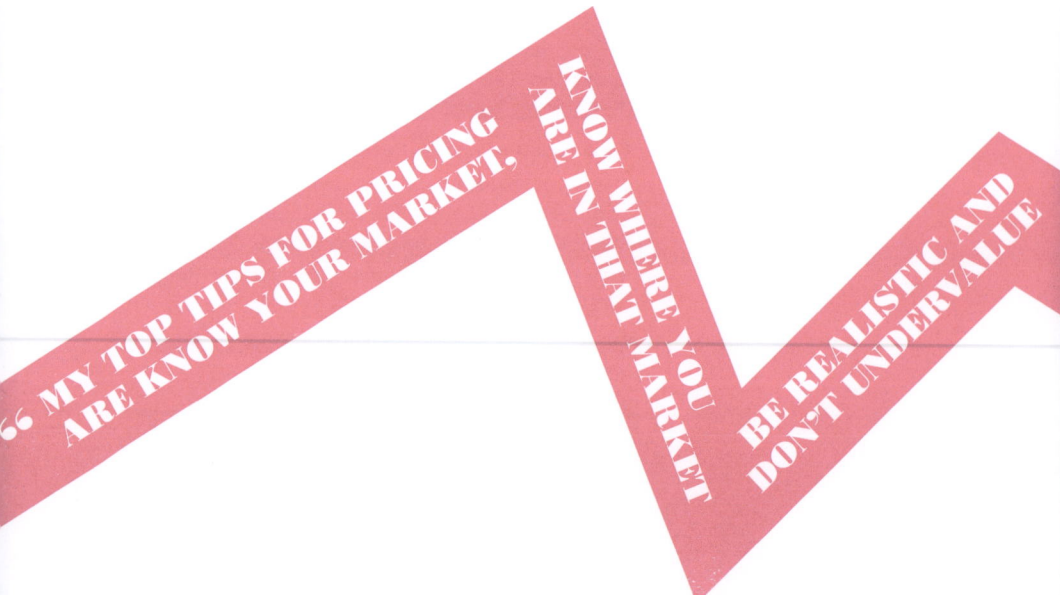

" MY TOP TIPS FOR PRICING ARE KNOW YOUR MARKET, KNOW WHERE YOU ARE IN THAT MARKET, BE REALISTIC AND DON'T UNDERVALUE

05

03 Price

The price of the product or service generates income and, most importantly, profit, whilst all the other elements in the marketing mix incur costs. It is vital that you understand the relationship between price, cost and profit.

This is outlined below.

What it costs to make including time, materials and overheads

What you can charge in the market place based on <u>value</u> and cost

= Price – Cost

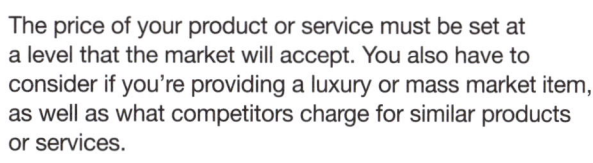

Johanna Basford,
Designer / Illustrator

The price of your product or service must be set at a level that the market will accept. You also have to consider if you're providing a luxury or mass market item, as well as what competitors charge for similar products or services.

If it's too expensive it may not sell as the benefits to the customer are not acknowledged. On the other hand, a product that's too cheap may not produce a sufficient return to cover costs and sustain the business. A low price may also infer it's poor quality or inferior.

The price of your product or service must include both the costs to produce it and the additional costs associated with selling it, as discussed in Place.

www.nesta.org.uk

06

THE MARKETING MIX

04 Promotion

To choose the appropriate means of promoting your product or service you need to consider who your customer is and how you will reach them.

Market segmentation is where you divide your overall target market into smaller sub-markets made up of people with the same needs. This allows you to target them in the right way.

For example, if your target market is householders to whom you wish to market an energy monitoring device, then you might look at sub-markets of age. Are elderly people more likely to want the product to help control energy bills? Are younger householders more likely to want it because they're concerned about environmental issues? This type of research can help you develop marketing messages and use marketing methods appropriate for these sub-markets.

When looking at sub-markets, you could divide your consumer markets using the following profiles:

- **Behaviour**: usage, frequent/infrequent, favourable impressions, convenience

- **Character**: lifestyle, personality, trendsetter/follower

- **Socio economic factors**: profession, income, location, buying patterns/loyalty, age and gender

If you are segmenting a business market, you could consider the following component parts:

- **Company size**: small, medium or large

- **Industry type**: IT, finance, education, media, local government

- **Location**: local, Scotland, UK, Mainland Europe

Marketing and Promotional Tools

Having established facts about your product and the relevant markets, you need to consider how to get your business and product noticed.

Not every method of communication will be right for your business. And the methods you use can change as your business develops and grows.

Before engaging in any promotional activity you need to be clear:

- What message do you want to communicate?
- Who is the audience?
- What is the best way to communicate with them?
- What budget do I have?
- What measures will I use to know if I have been successful?

Some promotional activities are expensive and should only be considered for specific products or markets and at certain points in the product lifecycle. There would be little point in spending thousands of pounds on advertising in a glossy magazine if your customers tend to buy your product via the internet.

The six main tools for promoting your business and product or service are:

- Public Relations
- Advertising
- Internet & Online Marketing
- Direct marketing
- Sales promotion
- Personal Selling

08

THE MARKETING MIX

Public Relations

Public Relations (PR) is about creating and maintaining an image for your business or product that's the essence of its values and integrity, and that forms your reputation.

The impression you make through press coverage is highly visible and long-lasting. It's therefore important that you try to control the range and content of press stories about your business.

If you choose to communicate with the media through press releases it's essential the information contained in these is newsworthy. Just because you think something about your company or product is interesting doesn't necessarily make it a news story. It has to be of sufficient interest or importance to the public or sections of the public to warrant coverage in the media, e.g. a new product or person, an investment, or a new contract.

Writing endless press releases and sending them to nameless editors and journalists on a database of press outlets is not the way to get good coverage. Likewise, If you send out releases each week simply to keep your profile up, then you are in danger of damaging your reputation.

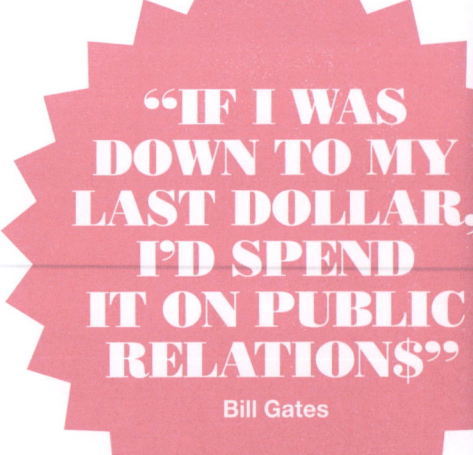

"IF I WAS DOWN TO MY LAST DOLLAR, I'D SPEND IT ON PUBLIC RELATION$"
— Bill Gates

09

Journalists receive hundreds of press releases each day, so it's important to target the right journalists with information relevant to their area of interest.

If you can't afford professional PR support, then the SOLAADS rules can help you to get your message across in a press release.

Subject   What is the subject of the story?

Organisation   Which organisation is the story from?

Location   Where is it located?

Advantages   What advantages to public and/or company does this story encapsulate?

Applications   What does the subject of this story do and who can use it or benefit from it?

Details   What are the precise details (if about a person, their biographical details or if it is about a product, its dimensions, size, scale etc)?

Source   Who issued the press release and what are their contact details?

Using SOLAADS rules can help you focus on telling the story. Other tips for writing a press release are to include all the key components of the story in the first paragraph. That way, if a news editor reads your press release their interest will be invoked right away and they'll have all the relevant facts.

www.nesta.org.uk

10

THE MARKETING MIX

Advertising

There are three main reasons for advertising:

- To create awareness among your target audience
- To persuade customers to buy your product by promoting its benefits
- To keep up your company profile.

To be effective, any advertising undertaken by your business needs to be done regularly and have a recognisable tone. Advertising, whether TV, press or radio, can be expensive and is generally brokered by agencies that will charge for their time and input on top of any design, airtime and production costs.

Newspaper and magazine advertising costs vary with the type of publication, circulation and readership figures and the size and position of the advert.

Advertising on the internet is generally cheaper than other forms. You can advertise on Google by yourself without an intermediary.

An online advert can be changed quickly and easily, but pop-up adverts can be considered intrusive and annoying. Online advertising can improve your search engine rankings, increase awareness of the product and entice browsers from other websites to yours.

The impact of advertising is difficult to track unless you include a monitoring tool like a voucher or coupon promotion in print. Online advertising can be tracked through hits to your advert or site, but this might not necessarily correspond with an increase in sales.

11

Internet and Online Promotion

A well-designed and managed website can allow a company of any size to reach customers all over the world. It can contain a variety of information in the form of press releases, news items, product information and products for sale. It's important to maximise your search engine ranking and build links on and to partner websites.

If you plan to sell your product or service online, then the architecture and functionality of your site must allow you to meet promises and fulfil orders. Make sure to invest in planning and testing your website – those who do then spend around two thirds less time fixing problems than those who don't (Source: Accenture).

Direct Marketing

- **Direct Mailing** can be a useful tool in business-to-business marketing, allowing you to personalise and target communications. But be careful when sending it to consumers – you don't want to be seen as 'junk mail', or be lost among it. To be effective, regularly update your databases. Use your own research, or buy up-to-date target lists from reliable sources.

- **Telemarketing** can promote, sell or solicit a product or service. You can gather information about potential business-to-business customers allowing you to build a comprehensive and up-to-date database of actual and potential customers. You can also use it to follow up on potential customers that you have emailed, written to or leafleted.

12

THE MARKETING MIX

— **Email marketing** has the advantage of being immediate, cost-effective and highly targeted. Emails can be tracked using specific software, indicating when it was opened and what links the user clicked on. It's best to avoid sending attachments as they may get blocked by the recipient's server or the recipient may be reluctant to open it.

It is critical to send emails only to those people who have at some stage agreed to receive information from you, for example, if they have signed up for a newsletter, are a previous customer, or made an enquiry about your product. There are strict legal implications governing the use of emails and it is imperative that you adhere to the EU directives on opting out of further communication issues. Business start up organisations in your area should be able to advise on this matter. A list of such organisations is provided in the Destinations section of handbook 01.

Sales Promotion

This can be described as short-term activities to encourage customers to buy, and boost sales for a limited period of time. This could include price reductions, money off vouchers, multi-buys, interest free credit, and extended guarantees. However, consistent discounting can damage the image of a product or service.

Personal Selling

Face-to-face marketing enables you to listen to prospective or existing customers needs and it allows you to convey the ethos and values of your business. This personal interaction also offers a valuable opportunity to get first-hand feedback on our products, your company and your competitors.

05 People

You and the people you employ are the biggest assets in your business. You will want to portray a positive image and keep your customers happy. Customer care and aftersales should be a priority for you to build your brand and ensure customer loyalty.

06 Process

The procedures that your company uses to deliver your product or service will have an effect on the customer. From supplying product information, providing quotations, taking an order, availability of stock, to tracking an order and delivering the product or service, each step is an opportunity to make a good or bad impression. Having high standards of customer care that are regularly monitored and reviewed will help you to deal effectively with any process issues and complaints.

07 Physical Environment

It is important that your workplace sets the right impression to your customers, suppliers and staff.
If the business appears shabby and untidy then potential customers may be put off. If customers have access to your premises then ensure that public areas reflect the values and character of the business.

You should also manage your image including updating your website. Having simple rules for any company promotional material – whether printed or electronic – should ensure a consistent image. This could include standardising the position of your logo, company name, corporate colours, and typeface used for all materials. Use worksheet 04a: Marketing Mix to explore the 7P's of marketing for your business.

14

THE MARKETING PLAN

Developing a Marketing Plan

A marketing plan is a clearly defined, detailed route to delivering your marketing strategy and should mirror the objectives contained in your business plan.

There are six elements to any Marketing Plan, some of which we've covered previously. They are:

01 Mission Statement
02 SWOT Analysis
03 Marketing Objectives
04 Marketing Strategies
05 Implementing the Plan
06 Measuring and Controlling the Plan

01 Mission Statement

The mission statement is a clear, concise summary of why your business exists and its future intentions. This was covered in handbook 02: Getting off the ground.

02 SWOT Analysis

This summarises the strategic positioning of your company. Refer to the SWOT analysis you conducted, also in handbook 02.

03 Marketing Objectives

Your marketing objectives should be based on your business strengths and weaknesses, and form a key part of your business plan and be set to specific timescales. They should be:

- **Definite:** e.g. to increase sales by 10%
- **Quantifiable:** to increase sales by 10%
- **Achievable:** you should have sufficient staff and financial resources to meet the objectives
- **Realistic:** it should be possible to meet the targets
- **Time sensitive:** timescales and deadlines should be set

04 Marketing Strategies

Marketing strategies are the means through which the marketing objectives are reached.

They are informed by the 7Ps: Product USP, the Place you will sell it, the Price you will charge, how you will Promote it, the People you involve, the Process you employ to make, sell and deliver it and the Physical Environment you operate from.

05 Implementing the Plan

The marketing plan states:

- Your intentions
- How each of the objectives will be achieved, and
- By what means.

To help you plan and guide your activities create a Critical Marketing Tasks Chart. This lists all the activities to be carried out, along with associated deadlines and individuals responsible for achieving them. Costs of carrying out the activities will be included in a budget.

16

THE MARKETING PLAN

An example is shown below. Use Worksheet 04b: Critical Marketing Tasks to help you devise and implement your marketing plan.

Activity	Timescales	Assigned to	Budget	Review
Launch company newsletter	April 2010	Ann	£500	Feedback from customers
Email Campaign	May 2010	John Part time contractor	4 Hours at £25 per hour	Response from customers
Trade Exhibition Edinburgh	Sept 2010	Sales person (Jane)	£2400 + travelling expenses	Number of sales and value of sales leads

06 Measure and Control the Plan

As with your business plan, you should regularly monitor and review the progress of your marketing activities, both in terms of staff resources and budgets. It's a good idea to have one person acting as project manager to chase up work in progress and monitor results. Any deviation in progress or finances should be acted upon and the marketing plan amended accordingly. A good Critical Marketing Tasks Chart combined with clear financial information will allow the plan to be effectively monitored and reviewed.

FINANCIAL MODELLING

The business decisions you make will always have financial impacts. Some will have a lot more than others. Where you locate your business, how you price your product or service, who you use as suppliers and how much advertising you do will all have important financial consequences.

To be in full control of your business, you need to be aware of the financial impacts of decisions before you make them, and also how changes in the business environment will impact on your enterprise. You will also need to measure the performance of your business, in terms of profit or the surplus that you've made after deducting your wages, overheads and costs.

> "It's taken me a while to get over my belief that you have to be on the breadline to be running a successful creative business. Now I realise it is about making money… we sell designs, we make money, then we can be more creative and take on more new projects!"

Johanna Basford, Designer / Illustrator

Consider your answers to the following questions. These deal as much with your lifestyle as your work or creativity. Your views are likely to change with time.

- How much money do I want to earn a year?
- How hard do I want to work?
- How do I feel about employing others or working with partners?
- What is my attitude to taking risk?
- How self-disciplined am I likely to be in building my business?

18

FINANCIAL MODELLING

These next questions are about the size and capacity of your business.

- What annual turnover (this is your sales in one year) would make me feel my business is properly established?
- What do my competitors charge for their service or product?
- What do I want to charge for my service or product?
- How am I going to generate the sales I need?

> "I used these creative techniques to explore how I shape my fledgling business but I know that unless I'm making money it's not a business at all."

Carrie Ann Black, Contemporary Jeweller

To get a complete view of your decisions and the possible consequences of them, you also need to consider your business costs. These are split into two categories: direct costs and indirect costs.

Direct Costs

These are the costs that you incur as a direct result of making a product or selling a service, for example raw material costs, labour and advertising costs. Consider the following:

- If my business makes and sells products, what are the direct costs (materials, labour, distribution, design, advertising and marketing) of producing one unit of each product?
- If my business is a service business, how much will I charge for my time and how much of it will I need to spend developing and marketing the services I am offering?

Indirect Costs or Overheads

These are the costs that you and your business incur even if you produce or deliver nothing. Consider the following:

- How much do I want to pay myself as a salary?
- Where will my business be located and what costs will that incur (such as rent, phones, broadband, insurance, utilities and business rates)?
- What professional services (such as lawyers and accountants) will I need? What will they cost?
- How much will other items (such as postage and stationery) cost?
- How much will I have to pay other consultants to deliver my product or service?

You may also have to spend money on equipment, such as machinery or computers, which the business will then own as an asset. This is known as Capital Expenditure or Capital Investment. Consider the following:

- How much will I need to invest in equipment (such as computers or machinery)?

It may be some time before you start to make a profit. In the meantime, your business will need to be financed in some way. Borrowing from friends and family, loans or a bank overdraft are the most common ways of bridging the gap. So consider:

- How will my business be financed in the period before it begins to make profits?
- How long will this period be?

20

FINANCIAL MODELLING

All businesses face risks of various kinds, such as the risk of losing business to competitors, having a supplier go out of business, or transport costs increasing. It's critical to be aware of the risks your business may face. Consider the following:

- What are the main risk factors that affect/determine the basic profitability of my business? (These may be things such as competitors changing their prices, supply bottlenecks or ineffective marketing).

- How sensitive to each of these factors is my business?

These questions can seem daunting, and it's important to remember that the aim isn't to come up with a set of perfect answers! There's no such thing – no-one can predict the future. The questions are there to help you think about the financial consequences of your decisions and to pre-empt the sorts of questions other people, such as your bank manager, are likely to ask you about your business. You can experiment with different pricing structures, sales forecasts and marketing costs to see the impact of each of these.

If you would like help with this you can contact your local business support service for advice and information – see Destinations in handbook 01 for a list of useful contacts.

Cash Flow

Cash flow shows how much money is coming in and out of your business at any one time. If you understand your cash flow then you know when you're likely to have bills coming in and, most importantly, whether you'll have enough money to pay them. By working out your cash flow, you can identify possible problems in advance and decide what you might do about them.

Refer back to your Blueprint Model to help you think about your business's cash flow. In the blueprint you identified operational activities in a time frame. Each of those activities will have to be resourced, and those resources will have a cost. By entering those costs as outgoings and entering values for income generated by onstage activity in a time frame, you can start to work out a basic cash flow. A 12-month time frame showing monthly income and expenditure helps identify seasonal variations in sales and costs.

In diagram 01 you can see the various categories of money flowing in and out of a business.

Money In:

- Sales revenues.

- Financial investments (such as grants, loans and equity investors).

- Interest on surplus cash.

Money Out:

- Direct production costs if you are a product based company (these cover things such as materials, labour, packaging, advertising – anything that is linked directly to making and selling your products).

- Indirect costs (such as rent, utility bills, insurance and any other costs that you incur whether or not you sell your product or services).

- Capital investment (including buying items such as computers, machinery or equipment).

- Loan repayments and dividends (this is repaying any loans you may have and paying dividends from profits to any investors you have).

22

FINANCIAL MODELLING

Diagram 01 Basic cash flow process.

Note that the illustration does not deal with Value Added Tax (VAT), or Corporation Tax, should your business generate sufficient revenue.

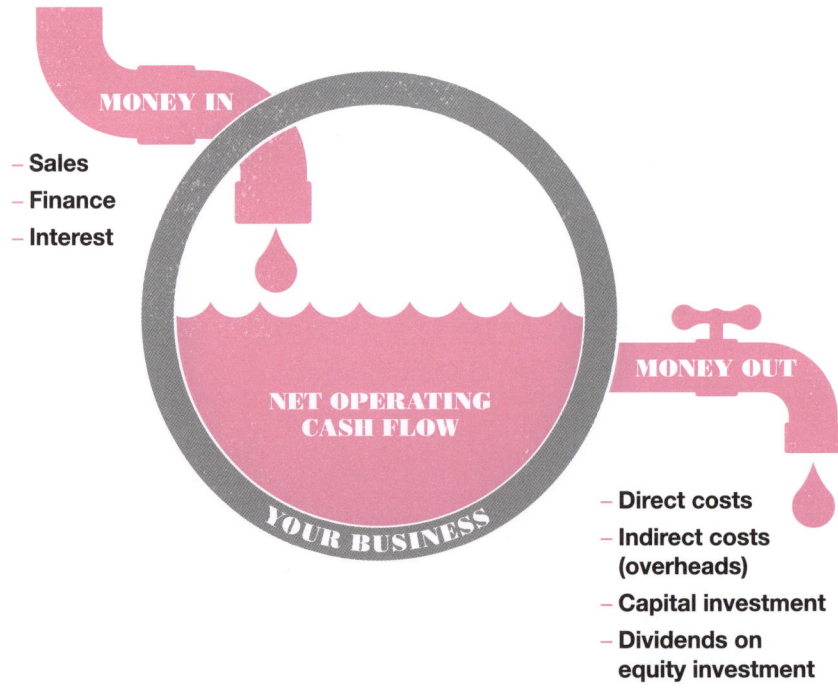

MONEY IN
- Sales
- Finance
- Interest

NET OPERATING CASH FLOW

YOUR BUSINESS

MONEY OUT
- Direct costs
- Indirect costs (overheads)
- Capital investment
- Dividends on equity investment

23

Developing a Cash Flow

A cash flow spreadsheet in Excel for an imaginary business that makes and sells products, and also generates income from licences and services is shown on pages 26 and 27. It could be a designer who makes and sells their own pieces and also acts as a consultant to other companies. (Your Customers and your Relationship Model will have identified the types of income streams for your business.) You can use a similar format to develop a cash flow for your business.

Your cash flow should include:

- Light grey area: **Cash Inflows**
  In this example there are three: product sales, license income and consultancy services. Sales volume and price assumptions and the first month that sales are assumed to be made are included. Grant finance, along with a loan that has been arranged is shown as other funding

- Light red area: **Cash Outflows or Costs**
  Some assumptions have been made about direct costs per unit of output and the main categories of indirect costs. The amount to be spent on capital equipment (vehicles, machinery and computers, etc) and the month of expenditure.

- Dark grey area: **Finance Costs / Receipts**
  There are assumptions for the average interest rate received on positive cash balances in the business account and those paid on any overdraft balances.

24

FINANCIAL MODELLING

The projections are monthly for the first year and annually for the two subsequent years. This gives a more detailed picture for the short term, enabling possible cash flow problems to be identified and remedied quickly, while providing enough of a longer-term picture to get a feel for the business's true commercial potential.

Spreadsheets for calculating cash flow are available from your local business support service or bank manager. By changing the input assumptions and noting the consequences of these in terms of the cash flow, you'll get an idea of what different changes could mean for your business.

Getting the Numbers to Add Up

Building up a picture of your cash flow and modelling the consequences isn't easy. You need to make sure, as much as possible, that your assumptions about the market are correct. People often underestimate the amount of time it takes to get people to start buying their product or service and overestimate the amount of sales they'll make. The more research you do, the more accurate your assumptions are likely to be.

At this very early stage, it may feel that you're making up the numbers. You might not know how many products you will sell in your first year of trading, but it's useful to make your best guess. However, as soon as you've started the business you're going to generate numbers that will be more accurate and meaningful. It'll be important to record these numbers as soon as they're available, so you can begin to see how your business is performing.

It might be useful to remind yourself of the difference between cash flow, profit and loss and balance sheet:

- Cash flow: shows the movement of cash into and out of the business at the time it occurs.

- Profit and Loss: is an accounting view of the profits or losses earned by the business on the date an invoice is raised (rather than payment made as per the cash flow) over a particular period of time such as a quarter or year. It also includes a number of non-cash items such as depreciation on fixed assets.

- Balance Sheet: is a snapshot of the assets and liabilities of the business on a given date.

Dealing with financial matters might seem scary or boring, but by understanding your cash flow you will know what you're earning, what you owe and, vitally, whether you're making any money.

As a starting point it might be useful to create a 'survival budget' to help you assess what it costs you to live each month/year. Add up all of your living costs e.g. rent/mortgage, utility services, council tax, credit card payments, car and living expenses. By calculating this you will know how much money you need to earn through your business in order to make it survive and grow - this will allow for better financial planning in the future.

By putting in place financial systems that are reviewed regularly and that empower you to know how well your business is operating you will ensure its sustainability.

FINANCIAL MODELLING

Cash Flow Projection Example

Cash Flow Projections	Jan 10	Feb 10	Mar 10	Apr 10	May 10	Jun 10	Jul 10
Cash Inflows							
Product Sales	£0	£0	£0	£0	£0	£0	£3,000
Licensee royalties	£0	£0	£0	£2,000	£2,000	£2,000	£2,000
Consulting income	£0	£0	£0	£0	£0	£0	£0
Business bank loan	£0	£0	£0	£8,750	£0	£0	£8,750
Start-up grant	£8,750	£0	£0	£0	£0	£0	£0
Workshop delivery - teaching	£5,000	£0	£0	£0	£0	£0	£0
Total Cash Inflow	**£13,750**	**£0**	**£0**	**£10,750**	**£2,000**	**£2,000**	**£13,750**
Cash Outflows							
Direct Costs							
Materials	£0	£0	£0	£0	£0	£0	-£960
Direct Labour	£0	£0	£0	£0	£0	£0	-£600
Delivery / Postage	£0	£0	£0	£0	£0	£0	-£60
Marketing	£0	£0	£0	£0	£0	£0	-£500
Total Direct Costs	**£0**	**£0**	**£0**	**£0**	**£0**	**£0**	**-£2,120**
Overheads							
Salary	-£1,000	-£1,000	-£1,000	-£1,000	-£1,000	-£1,000	-£1,000
Office / Shop rent	-£700	-£700	-£700	-£700	-£700	-£700	-£700
Software / Web Service	-£15	-£15	-£15	-£15	-£15	-£15	-£15
Telephone	-£50	-£50	-£50	-£50	-£50	-£50	-£50
Utilities	-£50	-£50	-£50	-£50	-£50	-£50	-£50
Travel	-£200	-£200	-£200	-£200	-£200	-£200	-£200
Printing	-£15	-£15	-£15	-£15	-£15	-£15	-£15
Equipment rentals	-£25	-£25	-£25	-£25	-£25	-£25	-£25
Accounting	-£75	-£75	-£75	-£75	-£75	-£75	-£75
Legal	-£40	-£40	-£40	-£40	-£40	-£40	-£40
Insurance	-£15	-£15	-£15	-£15	-£15	-£15	-£15
Repairs / Maintenance	-£20	-£20	-£20	-£20	-£20	-£20	-£20
Supplies - Office	-£15	-£15	-£15	-£15	-£15	-£15	-£15
Postage	-£15	-£15	-£15	-£15	-£15	-£15	-£15
Bank Charges	-£5	-£5	-£5	-£5	-£5	-£5	-£5
Training and Development	-£50	-£50	-£50	-£50	-£50	-£50	-£50
Other	-£30	-£30	-£30	-£30	-£30	-£30	-£30
Total Overheads	**-£2,320**	**-£2,320**	**-£2,320**	**-£2,320**	**-£2,320**	**-£2,320**	**-£2,320**
Capital Expenditure							
Vehicles	£0	£0	£0	£0	-£4,000	£0	£0
Machinery and Equipment	£0	£0	-£1,000	£0	£0	£0	£0
Computers and other IT	£0	£0	£0	£0	-£3,000	£0	£0
Total Capital Expenditure	**£0**	**£0**	**-£1,000**	**£0**	**-£7,000**	**£0**	**£0**
Finance Costs / Receipts							
Repaid loans: OUT	£0	£0	£0	£0	£0	£0	£0
Interest paid / (received)	£0	£29	£23	£15	£36	£18	£17
Total Finance Costs	**£0**	**£29**	**£23**	**£15**	**£36**	**£18**	**£17**
Total Cash Outflow	-£2,320	-£2,291	-£3,297	-£2,305	-£9,284	-£2,302	-£4,423
Net Cash Flow	£11,430	-£2,291	-£3,297	£8,445	-£7,284	-£302	£9,327
Opening Bank Balance	£0	£11,430	£9,139	£5,842	£14,287	£7,003	£6,701
Closing Bank Balance	£11,430	£9,139	£5,842	£14,287	£7,003	£6,701	£16,028

In it for the long haul Speaking to customers and staying in business

Aug 10	Sep 10	Oct 10	Nov 10	Dec 10	Total Year 1	Year 2		Year 3	
					% change	Assumed Amount	% change	Assumed Amount	
£3,000	£3,000	£3,000	£3,000	£3,000	£18,000	10%	£19,800	25%	£24,750
£2,000	£2,000	£2,000	£2,000	£2,000	£18,000	50%	£27,000	25%	£33,750
£0	£700	£700	£700	£700	£2,800	0%	£2,800	25%	£3,500
£0	£0	£8,750	£0	£0	£26,250	0%	£0	0%	£0
£0	£0	£0	£0	£0	£8,750	0%	£0	0%	£0
£0	£0	£0	£0	£0	£5,000	0%	£0	0%	£0
£5,000	**£5,700**	**£14,450**	**£5,700**	**£5,700**	**£78,800**		**£49,600**		**£62,000**
-£960	-£960	-£960	-£960	-£960	-£5,760	5%	-£6,048	5%	-£6,350
-£600	-£600	-£600	-£600	-£600	-£3,600	5%	-£3,780	5%	-£3,969
-£60	-£60	-£60	-£60	-£60	-£360	5%	-£378	5%	-£397
-£500	-£500	-£500	-£500	-£500	-£3,000	5%	-£3,150	5%	-£3,308
-£2,120	**-£2,120**	**-£2,120**	**-£2,120**	**-£2,120**	**-£12,720**		**-£13,356**		**-£14,024**
-£1,000	-£1,000	-£1,000	-£1,000	-£1,000	-£12,000	5%	-£12,600	5%	-£13,230
-£700	-£700	-£700	-£700	-£700	-£8,400	5%	-£8,820	5%	-£9,261
-£15	-£15	-£15	-£15	-£15	-£180	5%	-£189	5%	-£198
-£50	-£50	-£50	-£50	-£50	-£600	5%	-£630	5%	-£662
-£50	-£50	-£50	-£50	-£50	-£600	5%	-£630	5%	-£662
-£200	-£200	-£200	-£200	-£200	-£2,400	5%	-£2,520	5%	-£2,646
-£15	-£15	-£15	-£15	-£15	-£180	5%	-£189	5%	-£198
-£25	-£25	-£25	-£25	-£25	-£300	5%	-£315	5%	-£331
-£75	-£75	-£75	-£75	-£75	-£900	5%	-£945	5%	-£992
-£40	-£40	-£40	-£40	-£40	-£480	5%	-£504	5%	-£529
-£15	-£15	-£15	-£15	-£15	-£180	5%	-£189	5%	-£198
-£20	-£20	-£20	-£20	-£20	-£240	5%	-£252	5%	-£265
-£15	-£15	-£15	-£15	-£15	-£180	5%	-£189	5%	-£198
-£15	-£15	-£15	-£15	-£15	-£180	5%	-£189	5%	-£198
-£5	-£5	-£5	-£5	-£5	-£60	5%	-£63	5%	-£66
-£50	-£50	-£50	-£50	-£50	-£600	5%	-£630	5%	-£662
-£30	-£30	-£30	-£30	-£30	-£360	5%	-£378	5%	-£397
-£2,320	**-£2,320**	**-£2,320**	**-£2,320**	**-£2,320**	**-£27,840**		**-£29,232**		**-£30,694**
£0	£0	£0	£0	£0	-£4,000		-£1,000		-£1,000
£0	£0	£0	£0	£0	-£1,000		£0		£0
£0	£0	£0	£0	£0	-£3,000		-£2,000		-£2,000
£0	**£0**	**£0**	**£0**	**£0**	**-£8,000**		**-£3,000**		**-£3,000**
£0	-£400	-£400	-£400	-£400	-£1,600		-£3,400		£0
£40	£42	£44	£68	£70	£402		£871		£916
£40	**-£358**	**-£356**	**-£332**	**-£330**	**-£1,198**		**-£2,529**		**£916**
-£4,400	-£4,798	-£4,796	-£4,772	-£4,770	-£49,758		-£48,117		-£46,802
£600	£902	£9,654	£928	£930	£29,042		£1,483		£15,198
£16,028	£16,628	£17,530	£27,184	£28,112	£0		£29,042		£30,525
£16,628	£17,530	£27,184	£28,112	£29,042	£29,042		£30,525		£45,723

www.nesta.org.uk

28

BEFORE WE MOVE ON

The information and examples in this handbook have allowed you to explore how you might communicate with your customers, how you should plan any communications activity and how to deal with financial aspects of your business. To summarise:

- The Marketing Mix provides a framework to consider the key elements that should be in place for you to connect with you customers. These are the 7Ps of Marketing: Product, Place, Price, Promotion, People, Process and Physical Environment.

- You can develop a Marketing Plan that will allow you to prepare your communications strategy to ensure you maximise the impact of any information you send out.

- Financial Modelling introduced the vital role of finance to allow you to control your business activities. This is crucial for you to anticipate problems that might arise, and to ensure that your business doesn't lose money.

- Cash Flow is a tool to let you understand how money flows into and out of the business. By understanding this you can be in real control of your business finances to ensure you keep a healthy and sustainable business that meets your aspirations.

Now you have the main tools to shape, define, explain, communicate and control your business. But this is just the start of the journey – now you have to make it work!

You will find information on different types of company structures and a list of organisations that can offer assistance and support with setting up your business in the Destinations section of handbook 01: Arrivals and Destinations.

In it for the long haul   Speaking to customers and staying in business